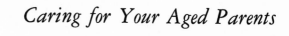

Caring for Your Aged Parents

Caring
for Your

BEACON PRESS   Boston

Aged Parents

Earl A. Grollman

Sharon Hya Grollman

Copyright © 1978 by Earl A. Grollman and Sharon Hya Grollman

Beacon Press books are published under the auspices
of the Unitarian Universalist Association

Published simultaneously in Canada by
Fitzhenry & Whiteside Ltd., Toronto

Printed in the United States of America

(hardcover)   9   8   7   6   5   4   3   2   1

Photograph by Steven Trefonides

Library of Congress Cataloging in Publication Data

Grollman, Earl A.
    Caring for your aged parents.
        1. Aged—United States—Family relationships.
2. Aged—Care and hygiene.   3. Parent and child.
I. Grollman, Sharon Hya, joint author.   II. Title.
HQ1064.U5G72   301.42'7   77–88384
ISBN 0–8070–2728–6

To Ray Bentley

our editor and friend

Contents

What This Book Is About

Few changes in life are as difficult to handle as the aging of our parents. The people who fed, clothed, and protected us may now be physically weak and emotionally dependent. The reversal of roles creates stress between the generations.

Grown children are very often unable to accept the changed circumstances without fear and resistance. Feelings of love and loyalty are mingled with anger and guilt. As a result, many decisions about elderly parents are often not the best ones. *Caring for Your Aged Parents* is written with the hope that you will understand your own reactions even as you try to comprehend your parents' needs.

We discuss a wide array of supportive community services for elderly parents still able to be independent. For those who cannot manage alone, we explore possible alternative housing arrangements, the question of parents' living with their children, and suggested criteria for choosing a nursing home, if that proves necessary. Most important, we emphasize that you and your parents can communicate effectively and work together creatively to solve your mutual problems.

A NOTE ABOUT THE FORMAT: You will notice that this book looks like poetry. We are not poets, but have used the format as a way of speaking in a direct, conversational tone and conveying useful information quickly and succinctly. In this way, we can say a great deal in very little space.

1. You—The Children of Aged Parents

"It won't happen.
My parents won't grow old,
need me,
depend on me.

"Other people's parents grow old.
Not mine."

You remember they said:

"Don't worry about us.
We'll never be a burden to you.
The last thing we'd do is
go to our children for help."

Their intentions were honest, but
the promises were unrealistic.

Your parents *do* need you.

And you are totally unprepared.

Now when you look at your parents
you are saddened.

The strong and comforting people
who once nurtured you
are now in need of
your strength and comfort.

The roles are reversed.

Your parents now seem like
your children:

> dependent,
> demanding,
> needing more, perhaps, than you can give.

In many ways, your children are
easier to handle.

The young grow up and
eventually care for themselves.

The painful reality is that your parents
probably won't get better
or need you less.

Unexpected reactions come
to the surface.

You find you still need their love,
and maybe resent that you weren't given
more of it.

Or you sense the loss of the strength
on which you once relied.

You must understand your
    disbelief,
    anger,
    guilt,
    panic,
    physical reactions,

if you are to deal
successfully with your emotions.

Disbelief

"My parents haven't changed.
(Not much anyway.)

"So they stumble once in a while.
(Probably need new glasses.)

"They forget to turn off the stove.
(Everyone makes mistakes.)"

You may make all kinds of excuses.

If you don't admit what's happening to them,
then it may not be true.

It's a way of saying,

"I don't want to think about it.
Not now, anyway."

Disbelief is often a first reaction to change,
a denial of painful events,
a defense against emotional involvement.

But pretending that nothing is wrong
may prevent you from seeking and finding
available help.

Anger

You are angry with yourself
for not being able to deal with
your parents without resentment.

You may be furious with your brothers
or sisters

for their unreasonable suggestions and
unjustified criticism of the way
you are handling the situation, and
for their seeming lack of understanding
of your personal circumstances.

Taking care of elderly parents can
create more internal strife among siblings
than the eventual reading of the will.

No matter how much you love your parents,
you may feel bitter.

When you ask:
"How much do I owe them?"
earlier memories are recalled:

they favored your brother or sister;
punished you when you were young, for things
        you hadn't done;
never cared for your spouse

"I never lived up to their expectations
then.
What do they expect of me
now?
     my time?
     my money?
     my life?"

You are caught in a trap:

How can you fulfill your
duty to your parents,
responsibility toward your spouse and children,
and the need to lead your own life?

You are frustrated and enraged
because you feel you
can't break out without
failing in one of these commitments.

Guilt

You raise your voice against your parents.

Later you resolve:

"It won't happen again."

The promise is soon forgotten.

You shout again and again.

You feel guilty.

"After all they've done for me."

You're ashamed of

> your "irrational" outbursts,
> your parents' feelings of disappointment in you,
> your embarrassment at the way they are now acting.

You're bruised by your conflicting emotions.

The more you feel you are
short-changing your parents,
the greater your self-recrimination.

Especially if, even for a moment,
you allow yourself to think:

"It would be easier for everybody
if they died."

You are not the only one to have had
such a thought.

Panic

You are overburdened.

Your mind is a jumble;
you can't concentrate on the tasks at hand.

If only you could run away, anywhere.

Human beings can tolerate almost
anything as long as they
have some hope that the situation will get better.

You think your parents will only get worse.

You feel hopeless.

Physical Reactions

Emotional stress affects your
physical well-being.

Perhaps you experience:
    exhaustion,
    headaches,
    insomnia,
feelings of emptiness in the stomach.

Each of these symptoms may occur alone,
or in any combination
or degree of intensity.

Accepting Your Emotions

You are not alone
in your anxiety and anguish.

The resentment, shame, and irritation
are indications of the pain
you are going through.

Accepting your reactions as natural
can help you resolve them.

Finding answers for your parents
and for yourself
is a long, painful process.

There are probably no solutions that will
satisfy everyone involved.

You can, however, choose the best one.

It will be worth the effort.

2. *Your Parents*

Your parents look in the mirror
and feel betrayed.

Old age is not the season of vanity.
Hair turns gray.
Skin is wrinkled.
The body is stooped.

It is as if they are ravaged
by an unseen enemy.

Physical Problems

Sometimes changes in outward appearance
are signs of physical infirmities.

Nearly nine out of ten elderly people
have one or more chronic health problems.

Most of the difficulties involve some loss
of motor or sensory abilities.

Some physical problems may be preventable.
Many can be treated and perhaps controlled.

Fortunately, most older people develop ways
to adapt to change.

Hearing

"I don't hear as well as I used to.
People have to shout and
repeat things.
I hope to God I'm not
going deaf."

Hearing loss is the most widespread
impairment associated with aging.

26

Your parents may use up so much energy
concentrating on listening,
straining to hear,
that they are exhausted
by the end of the day.

Loss of hearing is an invisible handicap.
Other people may think they just
aren't interested
or paying attention to what is
being said.

When people can't hear clearly,
they can't make accurate judgments.

Partial deafness can cause anxiety,
maladjustment, and isolation, creating
discomfort in group situations,
where noisy conversations interfere with
understanding what's being said.

Lack of understanding can cause
suspicion and paranoia.

There is an interaction between
loss of hearing and depression.

Suggest to your parents
that they have a complete hearing examination.

Rehabilitation programs providing the services of
        an audiologist (a nonmedical specialist trained
                in fitting hearing aids),
        a speech pathologist, and
        an otologist (ear doctor)
can determine the type of hearing loss.

Surgical intervention can be used to rectify
conductive loss, when the outer ear and
middle ear are closed off
by infection or allergy.

Hearing aids are often prescribed for
sensorineural loss, which involves damage to,
or malformation of the inner ear or auditory nerves.

Strangely, there is usually no difficulty in
convincing parents to use eyeglasses and dentures,
yet they often rebel against wearing hearing aids.

Try to convince them how pride
can prevent their getting
sorely needed assistance.

It will help for them to admit
that they just don't hear well,
and to say:

"I'm sorry.
I didn't hear you.
Will you say it again?"

There are ways to
confront the problem of hearing loss:

> a flashing lamp to replace a fire alarm system;

> inexpensive television attachments that increase
> the sound without disturbing other listeners;

> an adjustable wheel on the handset of the telephone,
> that amplifies the voice of the person on the
> other end.

When you talk to your hard-of-hearing parents:

Speak face-to-face in a well-lighted area, and
keep your hands away from your face.
Seeing your expressions will help them
interpret your words.

Speak in a normal fashion without shouting or
elaborately mouthing words.

Recognize that people don't hear so well
when they are tired or sick.

Dull ears don't mean a dull mind.

Vision

"For quite a while I pretended that
I was tired.
The lighting was poor.
But it's my eyes.
I just don't see well anymore."

Vision changes with age.

Muscles that control pupil dilation
for light adaption are altered.

There is a higher incidence of
glaucoma (increased pressure) and
cataracts (clouding of the lens).

Visual loss may discourage parents
from joining in social activities.
It may curtail or eliminate such pastimes as
reading, watching television, or doing handiwork.
It causes decreased mobility and poor orientation.

The label "senile" can be misused
for those unable to move effectively
because of poor vision.

A thorough eye examination could
determine whether stronger eyeglasses are needed
or corrective surgery is necessary.

Visual aids are readily available:

Large-print books, magazines, newspapers

Talking-book machines and records

Reader services

Low-vision aids from simple magnifying glasses
to telescopic eyeglasses

Sophisticated machinery that translates
print to raised letters
and print to spoken words

There are safety devices and precautions:

      Double-railed stairs

      Non-skid carpeting

      Better lighting

      Removal of obstacles in living quarters
          Objects *you* will notice
          may not be seen by your parents

Get advice:

Some states have a full range of services
available to the visually handicapped.

Balance and Equilibrium

The aging process involves changes
in the nervous system, in muscle tone,
reflex actions, and posture control.

Your parents may feel unsteady and dizzy;
they may walk slowly and with hesitation.

They may lose their balance and
fall frequently.

They may need more time than usual
to prepare to go out of the house.

Maybe you are taking them to the doctor.

They have their hats and coats on an hour before
the appointment, even though you've assured them
that the trip to the office will take fifteen minutes.

They call: "Why aren't you ready?"

It's their way of expressing anxiety about the visit,
about what they may learn from the doctor.

They need more time to walk to the car, to the elevator.

Understand their slower movement
and their need to adjust to it.

Some conditions require
a cane or walker for support,

or a wheelchair.
But remember that a person in a wheelchair
sees the world differently
from those standing upright.

The person has to look up to see.

Muscles are cramped.

Make sure that you always
tell your parent where and when
you are pushing the wheelchair.
Don't jolt their nerves and bodies.

Rehabilitation centers can provide your parents
with physical and occupational therapy
to improve their mobility and
increase their self-reliance.

Taste

"I'm not hungry.
Besides, the food tastes flat.
More salt, please."

Because older people's sense of taste
is less acute,
they often demand more highly
seasoned foods.

But this can be dangerous if they are on a
low-sodium or salt-free diet.

A nutritionist can help to plan
wholesome and palatable diets.

Sensation of Pain, Heat, Cold

There is a sharp decrease in ability
to identify sensations of pain.

Older people, aware of discomfort,
are often unable to isolate its source.
Something as localized as an ingrown toenail,
infected tooth, impacted bowel,
may not be recognized as such.

The frustration of feeling miserable
and not knowing the cause
may lead to irritability.

Thermal senses are impaired.

Unaware of the temperature of the bathwater,
older people may scald themselves.

On the other hand, they are more sensitive
to cold weather.

While everyone else is sweltering,
they grumble that the heat should be
turned up.

An extra sweater or blanket
might be all that's needed.

Sexuality

"Sexual joy is reserved for the young,
for those in the first decades of life."

"The elderly have no need for
sexual satisfaction."

"Especially after years of living alone,
they are sexually impotent."

"Physical intimacy is 'forbidden'
for people over sixty."

These statements are false
and misleading.

Society has misunderstood the
sexual interests of older people.

Sex life for the elderly is not inappropriate,
nor are those who have sex
"dirty old people."

Physical affection—holding, hugging, closeness—
are necessary and comforting
for the old as well as the young.

The elderly have the right to live
and to love as fully as they are able.

Memory

"I keep forgetting things.
Important dates.
Appointments.
Doctor's instructions.
Whether I turned off the stove.
Where I left my glasses.
People's names—my closest friends

"I feel as if I'm losing my mind."

Most older people experience
these changes to some degree.

What happened yesterday and today is hazy,
uncertain, sometimes completely forgotten.

Yet they recall past events with great accuracy.

There are many reasons
for memory problems:

> arteriosclerosis—the hardening and narrowing
>   of the arteries,
> side effects of medication,
> malnutrition,
> disorientation because of a new situation
>   or new surroundings,
> depression and anxiety.

Consult a physician.

Do not accept glib answers like
"What can you expect at that age?"
or
"A little confusion is normal
for this time of life."

A psychiatric evaluation
in conjunction with neurological tests
can help the doctor determine what the problem is.

Very often, the problem may be treatable,
but if nothing is done,
the damage could become permanent.

You can help your parents' memories by having them:

        associate a name with some event or person
            ("You remember, Connie brought you the cheesecake.");
        repeat unfamiliar names often
            ("Your new neighbors, the Kearns");
        write down the physician's instructions immediately
            ("The doctor said two pills four times a day;
            not four pills twice a day.")
use a large, clear calendar to mark their appointments.

An occasional telephone call helps to reinforce matters
that shouldn't be forgotten or overlooked,
and it reminds your parents that you care.

Losses

In addition to your parents'
memory loss and other physical changes,
the accumulation of years brings
with it an increase in psychological losses.

Old age has been referred to as
"the season of losses."

     For good reason.

Their Personal Losses

Your parents have a diminishing circle
of people who are important to them.

Death robs them of
siblings,
other relatives,
colleagues,
friends,
a spouse,
even—sometimes—their child.

Their Social and Financial Losses

The compensations of work are gone.

Not just the money,
but the self-esteem and satisfactions
that formed the structure
of their earlier years.

More time is spent at home.

Mother and father often get on each other's nerves.

Perhaps reluctant to participate in
outside social and recreational activities,
they create a self-imposed isolation.

They see themselves as being in the way,
on the fringes of life.

The Vicious Circle

In the aging process
one loss can lead to another:

  decline of physical health,
  decreased activity,
  lowered earning capacity,
  loss of independence,
  changes in relationships with family and friends,
  physical and social isolation,
  low self-esteem,
  depression,
  mental illness.

Old age can indeed be a losing game.

Mental Illness

"I sometimes wonder in the morning
if life is worth getting up for."

The pressures on your parents
—physical, emotional, social, and personal—
may be unbearable.

So many painful situations arise
just when they are least able
to cope with them.

And because mental impairment is regarded
as inevitable and irreversible in old people,
they rarely get the help they need.

Remembering brings a sharp pain.

"Most everyone I know is gone."

Your parents may be

    apathetic,
    ready to argue at the slightest excuse,
    suspicious of everyone—including you,
    complaining continually,
    confused, disoriented,
    reacting with exaggerated emotional outbursts
        that are out of proportion to the causes,
    unconcerned about personal hygiene,
    unable to experience pleasure.

Parents' emotional changes often evoke
feelings of anxiety and hostility
in their children.

You may express these feelings by saying,
"Snap out of it!"

It doesn't do any good.

Your irritation demonstrates an inability
to handle the stressful situation,
and pushes you and your parents
farther apart.

"All I have left is death."

Self-destruction may be
their solution to a life without hope.

Some warning signals may be

> *The Physical Attempt*
> Twelve percent of those who attempt suicide
> will try again and will succeed within two years.

> *Verbal Threat*
> Those who do take their lives
> often speak about it beforehand.

> *Slow Suicide*
> Death-oriented behavior includes
> self-starvation,
> refusal to follow doctor's prescriptions and orders,
> hazardous activity,
> voluntary seclusion.

For professional help contact:

> *The family physician*
> A starting point for medical help and for
> referrals to specialists and treatment resources.

> *A psychiatrist*
> For an assessment of emotional problems.

> *Mental health agencies*
> With trained social workers, clinical psychologists,
> and family counselors.

A family conference,
perhaps with a psychiatric social worker as mediator,
could help you understand your role
in assisting your parents.

Many psychological services are fully or partially funded
by personal insurance policies or Medicaid.

Drugs

Drug therapy can often combat
depression, the consequences of arteriosclerosis,
and slowed body and muscle movement.

Drug use can also become drug abuse
when the elderly are confused about
the proper directions to follow
or hoard old bottles without written directions.

Help them check their medicine cabinet.
Remove unmarked prescriptions and old medicines.

Have them keep a card containing
a list of medications, including

> dosage and frequency,
> reason for taking,
> prescribing physician,
> and names and phone numbers of doctors and relatives.

Have your parent ask the doctor
the purpose of the medication,
how long before the drug takes effect,
possible side effects, such as dry mouth,
        loss of appetite, drowsiness, nausea,
long-term consequences,
addictive possibilities.

Inform the physician of other medicines
your parents are taking.
A chemical stew could trigger
unexpected and dangerous reactions.

Antacids for an ulcer can inhibit the effect of an
antibiotic being taken to cure an infection.

Such foods as fruit juices and milk
may reduce the effectiveness of some medicines.

Alcohol combined with sedatives can be lethal.

Every drug has a potential for both
adverse reaction and therapeutic relief.

If you notice unusual side effects,
inform the doctor immediately.

Informed Consent

"Why should my parents
know what's wrong with them?
It would kill them.
They could never handle it."

Children may be sparing themselves,
not their parents.

Your fears are communicated by your own
discomfort, defensiveness, and flight.

When parents are aware of their problems,
they can participate in necessary decisions.

If they learn the truth later,
they may resent their doctor and
lose confidence in you.

The most awesome reality is
often preferable to uncertainty.

Dying and Death

Each experience with illness,
each realization that another faculty
is impaired,
activates your parents' conscious and
unconscious anxieties about dying.

They may think a great deal about
how much time they have to live.

Parents' worst nightmares may
not even be of death,
but of a long-term illness that

wipes out their financial resources,
makes them totally dependent on others,
condemns them to unending, excruciating pain,
suspends them indefinitely between life and death.

The elderly accept the certainty of death
more willingly than the young do.

Often, when older people want to share
their feelings about death,
their children change the subject
or dismiss it by saying:

"Don't even talk about it.
You have plenty of years ahead of you."

You may be uncomfortable knowing
not only that your parents will someday die,
but that you too will grow old and die.

Understand your parents' need to
reassess their past,
work through their present fears, and
feel assured that important details will be
        taken care of as they would want them to be.

By listening and sharing with them, together you may
understand more fully the meaning of life
as you accept the reality of death.

3. Parents—On Their Own

Perhaps you now have a clearer understanding
of your parents' losses—
both physical and emotional.

Remember, however, that an impairment
need not imply a disengagement from life.

Your parents may still be able to
live with purpose and meaning.

By changing the supports in their environment,
you can help them maintain as much
independence as possible.

Those who make the best adjustment to old age
are those who have outside interests,
pleasant social relations with friends and relatives,
and a role in society.

And, most important,
their own home,
with privacy and independence.

Having their own home affords
them a sense of

> *Autonomy:*
> the ability to live their lives
> in their own way

> *Intimacy:*
> the familiar scene, providing
> continuity and security

> *Identity:*
> the sense of pride and satisfaction
> in maintaining a sense of individuality.

But your parents may not be able to
take care of themselves completely.

You are concerned about their
        medical needs,
        nutrition,
        personal hygiene, and
        emotional well-being.

Is a nursing home the only solution?

Community Resources

An institution is not the only answer
for parents with special needs.

There are community-sponsored and
private organizations that offer
various kinds of help for
elderly people who want to remain in their homes.

Visiting Nurse Services

If your parents are
suffering from a chronic illness,
recovering from sickness, or
in need of bedside care,
you can contact a visiting nurse association.

Nurses will come regularly
to provide your parents with
medication and injections,
wound and bandage care,
blood pressure checks, and
physical therapy.

Because of the nurse's visits
hospitalization is shortened, and
vital medical needs are responsibly administered
in familiar surroundings.

Homemaker—Home Health Aide

A trained person, working under
the supervision of a nurse, social worker,
or other professional,
assists your parents in

> *homemaker services:*
> food shopping, personal errands, light housekeeping
>
> *hygienic duties:*
> giving baths, changing dressings, and
> helping with prescribed exercises
>
> *information and referral services:*
> providing emotional support in times of stress,
> with referral to appropriate resources.

Home-Delivered Meals

Prepared nutritious meals are delivered
directly to the homes of the elderly,
with perhaps a sandwich, fruit, and dessert
to be refrigerated for later in the day.

An added benefit is the social interaction
with concerned volunteers.

Telephone Reassurance Program

Volunteers call your parents
seven days a week
at convenient, prearranged times.

The caller
checks on the well-being of your parents, and
helps to mitigate their loneliness and to
relieve their fears.

And the certainty that the call will be made
alleviates your own anxiety about their having
a fall unattended or a sudden illness.

You know that emergency aid would be forthcoming.

Chore Services

This program provides

> *minor home repairs:*
> replacing fuses, fixing leaks,
> installing locks

> *heavy cleaning:*
> moving heavy furniture, washing
> windows, cleaning the basement

> *yard and walk maintenance:*
> snow removal and lawn cutting.

This service is recommended for those
capable of caring for themselves
but needing help in and around their homes.

Transportation and Escort Services

Transportation is provided for those
who need personal assistance to go to the
doctor, shopping center, bank, library,
senior citizens' center when

> public transportation is unavailable
> > or inaccessible

> special help is required to board and travel on
> > buses, subways, trains

> an escort is needed to secure a service and
> > ensure a safe return home.

Friendly Visitors Program

Volunteers visit your parents on a
regularly scheduled basis,
filling leisure hours with
card-playing, letter-writing, and
reading aloud.

The visitors will listen sympathetically
and try to help your parents
make their own decisions,
develop new interests,
revive old hobbies,
and strengthen their links with the outside community.

Senior Social Centers

Senior Social Centers give your parents
an opportunity
to leave the isolation of their home
and enjoy recreation with others.

Many centers offer:

> *group programs:*
> classes in bridge, yoga, indoor gardening,
>   arts and crafts
>
> *cultural recreation:*
> concerts, theater, field trips, visits to
>   historical sites
>
> *nutrition:*
> hot lunches, classes in proper food planning
>
> *counseling and referral:*
>
> psychological help, crisis intervention, and
>   referral to appropriate agencies.

Geriatric Day Care Centers and Hospitals

These centers are designed for older people who
have a combination of physical, mental, and social
limitations, but do not wish to be institutionalized.

Instead, they spend the day in a clinic, nursing home, or
hospital-based facility where
occupational and physical therapy,
psychotherapy, and medical services
are available.

Physical and psychological programs help
the elderly to remain functioning members
in their communities,
reducing family tension for their children
who are busy during the day.

Other Services and Activities

Efforts have been made
for the aged who are sick.

But little labor has been devoted
to those who are healthy,
to keep them that way
as long as possible,
and enhance the quality of their lives.

Work

"The sudden cessation of productive work and
earning power often leads to physical and
emotional deterioration and premature death."

American Medical Association

Retirement for many is not a reward;
it can be a painful time when people
may confront years with neither
direction or goals.

If your parents have both
the desire and ability to work,
there are sometimes opportunities for re-entering
the work force so that they can regain
financial security and personal fulfillment.

They may find work similar to what they did previously,
or develop an interest or hobby
that might blossom into a lucrative pursuit.

Knowledge, experience, and skills
do not disappear at sixty-five.

Volunteering

Volunteering is an opportunity for your parents to
put their skills to use,
learn new ones,
and come into contact with new people, ideas,
and challenges.

Many agencies incorporate positions for older volunteers
into their formal structure.

Volunteer possibilities exist in
schools,
hospitals,
day care centers,
religious and fraternal organizations,
senior citizens' clubs, and
homemaker services.

Many local newspapers have special sections
that describe volunteer opportunities and
activities in their communities.

The government also sponsors both volunteer
and employment programs.

Education

Some colleges, aware of the educational
and cultural needs of older adults,
offer courses at little or no tuition cost.

School may bring your parents
intellectual involvement,
cultural stimulation,
and a sense of life outside their homes.

Contact the nearest university or
adult education center in your area.

Creative Use of Leisure Time

Some people look forward
to their later years with optimism.

Old age can be both an end and a beginning

>   an end to job demands, clocks, schedules

>   a beginning for those things they always wanted to do
>   but had no time for

Help your parents take inventory,
defining present needs and future goals,
and exploring those activities that bring them
the highest enjoyment.

4. Parents—Living with Their Children

If one of your parents dies,
or becomes seriously ill
and requires long-term hospital care,
you may say to the other:

"You can't manage alone.
The house is too big for you.
Come live with us."

You may even consider saying this to both of them,
if you're afraid they can no longer manage on their own.

Wait.

Your intentions are good.

But your actions
may not necessarily be in the best interests of
your parents,
your spouse and children,
you.

Consider your parents' needs . . .

Do they want to live with you, or other relatives, and
give up part of their independence?

Will they be isolated in your home,
without the security of friends, organizations,
and familiar landmarks?

Is your house large enough
to give them their needed privacy?

There are many important factors to be weighed.

Your family's needs . . .

What kind of relationship does the family
have with your parents?

If you and your spouse are busy during the day,
can your parents manage alone in your house?

Are you willing or financially able
to obtain outside help?

A three-generation household is a big
responsibility for *every* member.

If your spouse doesn't agree willingly,
the arrangement probably wouldn't work.

And you . . .

How do you feel?

Examine your past relationship with your parents.

The themes played before in your family's history
may be repeated.

If guilt is your only motivation,
you will soon resent your parents
for intruding into your home.

Decisions must be predicated on more
than momentary guilt.

Encourage the other members of your immediate family
to share their feelings about the move.

You have a better possibility of
working out the arrangements satisfactorily
when everyone expresses honest emotions.

Of course,
include your parents in the decision-making.

Discuss frankly what you might expect of each other
in terms of
food preparation,
chores around the house,
finances.

When your friends come to visit,
are your parents to be included in the gathering?

Will your parents feel deserted
if you and your spouse want to go out alone?

Explain your needs.
Listen to theirs.

There must be mutual understanding.

Perhaps a trial period could be arranged,
to work out such details as:

>*Money*
>If they want to contribute,
>instead of paying rent,
>they might place funds
>in a special account for your children's education.

>*Meals*
>When they don't enjoy the food you're planning
>to serve, perhaps that is a good time
>for them to go out with a friend.

>*Transportation*
>Be willing to take your parents to homes of friends,
>the community center, or doctor's office.

Your parents might retain their old apartment
during the experimental period,

just in case.

If they are able,
allow them to share household responsibilities:
    washing dishes,
    cooking,
    repair work.

Asking them for help
may make them feel needed,

not like boarders.

Of course, your parents should have
their own room—a place in the house
to pursue their own interests,
without disturbing other family members
or being disturbed themselves.

Remember, they are not
your servants or babysitters.

Encourage them to
invite their friends into your home,
and to participate in activities outside the home.

There may be times when you feel
angry, cheated, violated
because of simple things like
a newspaper not returned to you intact,
the water faucet that is not turned off in the bathroom.
Even the sight of dentures may make you feel squeamish.

Or bigger issues like:
your spouse's resenting the new responsibilities,
your children's unhappiness with the "other parents"
        who advise and criticize,
your being treated like a child by the parents
        you have to take care of.

Allow

>*ample time*
>to determine whether the accommodation
>can be successful
>
>*open communication*
>for everyone to understand the issues involved.

"If there is separation of old
people from family life,
there is tragedy for both
young and old."
>*Margaret Mead*

5. Parents—In a Nursing Home

"If my parents stay in my house
for one more day
I think I'll have a nervous breakdown.

"But they can't manage alone.

"Is a nursing home the only solution?"

It depends.

Before making any decisions
examine the situation.

Are your parents
mentally alert,
able to care for their personal needs (shopping,
        food preparation, dressing),
ambulatory,
in need of continuous medical care?

Again,
there may be community resources
available to help them remain in their homes.

Check the alternatives.

Homes for the aged, apartments in sheltered housing,
retirement hotels and villages, and congregate
public housing offer such diverse services as

>   the serving of an evening meal,
>   registered nurses or a resident physician, and
>   recreational and cultural programs.

Your parents may live in these facilities,
with a degree of self-sufficiency,
under the watchful eye of concerned people.

Contact your local housing authority,
community development agency, or office on aging.

If community services are insufficient,
alternative housing inappropriate,
or your parents cannot obtain a major part
of their medical care,

a nursing home may be the only choice.

A nursing home?

"Oh, my God.
How can I do this to them?"

The decision to institutionalize
a loved one
is among the most difficult
anyone is ever required to make.

You may feel panic-stricken.

In desperation you think
you must make a decision.
Any decision would be an improvement
over the uncertainty.

But this is a time for exercising judgment,
not for a rash decision you may regret later.

If you have brothers and sisters,
discuss the situation with them.

If you act alone,
you may be blamed
for poor judgment and
lack of consideration.

Your siblings may suggest other alternatives
and even offer some financial assistance.

Your parents' participation and preparation
        are essential.

Talk *with* them,
not *at* them.

Don't tell them
what you have already decided.

Wait for those moments
when you are all rested, alert,
and able to share in the discussion.

Timing is critical.

Your tone should be gentle, conversational;
not demanding and argumentative.

You may have to explain the situation
again and again,
so that they can understand
the possible changes in their lives.

Be prepared
if your parents say:

"What are you doing to me?
A nursing home?
So you can wash your hands of me?
After all I've done for you.

"You promised
you'd never put me in one of those places."

They may regard the nursing home as
the last stop,
a kind of purgatory,
halfway between society and the cemetery.

You are blamed for
the irreversible deterioration of their bodies,
their inability to take care of themselves,
your seeming unwillingness to care for their needs.

Institutionalization may seem to them
tantamount to rejection.

You might tell them that
you understand their sadness and anxiety;
that you know how hard it is for them to move
        at this stage of their lives.

Assure them that you're not hurrying;
that no decisions will be made immediately
and there will be time for them to change
        their minds.
You are merely preparing for what may be necessary.

Remind them that not all nursing homes
are cold and impersonal.

You will need to learn about
your parents' financial situation.

The family attorney and accountant
could help you to evaluate
your parents' economic resources
by preparing an inventory of such assets as
  savings and checking accounts,
  real estate,
  pensions,
  fraternal or professional society benefits,
  insurance policies,
  trust agreements,
  veterans' benefits,
  Social Security.

Keep an account of all records
so that you avert any family problems
in the future.

The government can help with:

Medicare
A health insurance program that pays for a
portion of hospital care as well as for
skilled nursing facilities.
Included may be physician and health services,
therapy, medical supplies.
> Contact your local Social Security office
> for details.

Medicaid
For those in low-income brackets,
payments are made for physicians and
medical services, intermediate care facilities,
and skilled nursing facilities.
> Contact your local welfare department
> to see if your parents qualify.

Supplemental Security Income (SSI)
A federal program for those in need of
financial assistance, and for people who
are blind and disabled.
> Contact your local Social Security office
> for information.

To find out about suitable nursing homes,
ask for recommendations from
>doctors,
>social workers,
>clergy,
>local or state health departments,
>hospital or nursing home associations,
>senior citizens' groups,
>Social Security office,
>relatives,
>friends.

Your doctor can help you to match
your parents' needs
to the appropriate level of nursing home care.

The two types are:

> *Skilled Nursing Facility (SNFs)*
> twenty-four-hour nursing service
> for "convalescent" patients
> who require constant medical supervision

> *Intermediate Care Facility (ICFs)*
> less intensive medical care than that
> offered by SNFs, with a greater emphasis
> on social and rehabilitative services.

Some institutions offer both levels of care.

Before visiting a nursing home
you should call to
determine the level of care provided,
the financial arrangements, including
        Medicare and Medicaid,
and space availability.

Be sure that the home and administrator
are licensed by the state.

When you first walk into a nursing home,
you may be shocked.

Many people are in wheelchairs,
or use walkers.

Some seem disoriented,
feeble.

Your reaction may be,

"My parents don't belong here."

Don't dismiss a particular home because of
your first impression.

Look further.
See if some of the residents are alert,
communicating freely with staff
and one another.

If possible, come with your parents on several occasions.
Visit unexpectedly at mealtime
and during the activities period.

Notice whether

the atmosphere is warm and friendly;

the rooms are soundproof, properly heated,
air conditioned;

the area is likely to please your parents and is
located conveniently near family, friends, and
hospital;

medical professionals are in residence or on call;

there are physical, speech, and occupational therapy
services, individual and group recreational
activities, religious services, chaplains, beauty
shop, barber;

the food being served is both nutritious and tasteful;

the people look relatively contented
(women wearing make-up and men neatly
dressed are good signs).

Remember, no type of facility
can serve all people effectively.
You are looking for the one
best suited to *your* parents.

Interview the administrator,
head nurse, and social worker.
Do they visit the residents regularly;
know their names?
What is the proportion of trained
professionals and volunteers to residents?

Ask the relatives of the residents
for their opinions.

Talk to the residents themselves.

Don't depend on a single source
or be unduly influenced by
an administrator's bias,
a child's guilt, or
a parent's resentment.

Careful scrutiny of the facility
and staff is an important factor
in making the proper choice.

Take your parents to visit
before their formal admittance
so that they can become familiar with the
surroundings,
residents, and
staff.

Ease their transition by being
with them on admission day and
staying for a few hours until
they're settled.

After the initial adaptation period,
your phone calls,
letters, and
visits
will bring them comfort and reassurance.

Occasionally, if possible, you might take them to a
restaurant,
movie, and
to your home
for birthdays, holidays, or
just casual visits.

As nearly as possible,
provide them with the kind of love
that you would give them
if they were at home.

Entering a nursing home is
a time of major stress for your parents.

Don't ignore this fact,
or, on the other hand, underestimate
your parents' resilience in making
a satisfactory adjustment.

Moving to a new environment
may markedly improve their morale.

6. Care and Understanding

We feel different about life at seventy-five
from the way we do at forty-five.

Viewpoints change.

Interaction among family members
of varying ages can cause friction.

You might put aside your feelings for the moment,
and really try looking at your parents' situation
through their eyes.

Ask yourself, "How do they feel?"

Listening

If your parents feel that the whole world
is against them,
it is good for them to know that
some people are on their side.

You can demonstrate your concern and support
by listening to them,
especially if they have little contact
with others.

They need someone to talk to,
someone with whom they can safely share
feelings and thoughts.

Let them talk
without interruption,
even if they go off on tangents.
It is one way for them
to get things off their chests.

Yet be on guard against making them
speak about those matters
which are embarrassing and
distressing to them.

Don't gloss over their
complaints and worries with
cheerful clichés and
patronizing reassurances,
such as:

"I only hope I'm as healthy
as you when I'm your age.
Look, your friends are worse off
than you."

Pain is pain,
whatever the age of the person who feels it
and no matter how unfortunate others may be.

Sharing

As important as listening is,
so is your sharing your world with them.

Talk about your personal life,
news of the family,
and events in the community.

When you seek their advice,
they know that you value their judgment.

If they can help you with your problems,
they feel like parents again,
like people with something useful
to offer others.

Acknowledging

Have you ever noticed
that you sometimes make decisions for your parents,
such as ordering their meals at a restaurant
without asking their preference; or
in the doctor's office,
answering questions concerning *their* health?

Treating older parents like helpless individuals
can be psychologically devastating to them,
undermining their self-regard and assurance.

"A Soft Answer Turneth Away Wrath"

"I want to eat *now*."

You answer, "Can't you see I'm busy?"

"NOW. This minute."

You argue, but to no avail.

He still wants his food NOW.

Ask yourself what you are gaining.

After the ranting and raving,
your parent may still not
understand the situation.

Sometimes it is better to submit,
and take a few moments to
give him what he wants
and thus avoid conflict.

In many cases, troubled people
cannot always help what they are doing,
nor can they stop doing it even
when they are asked.

It may be futile to argue them down.

When you shout to make your point,
it is you who have lost control.

Try as gently as possible to decide
what you can and cannot expect of each other.

Laughing

A sense of humor is helpful
in times of stress.

The ability to laugh
when you're having trouble
is like bringing fresh flowers into the house
after winter has withered the garden.

Laughing at oneself
can encourage others to laugh
at themselves, too.

Approving

What person is immune to praise?

When parents' feelings are low,
your respect and admiration can raise them.

"Mom, Dad, I'm proud of you."

Notice what happens.

Praise reassures them
that they are still valued.

Touching

Touching is the most comforting
way of communicating,
a testimony to the
quality of one's feelings.

When words have been exhausted,
try holding your parents' hands
or embracing them.

Celebrating

How about a party after an operation or illness?

It praises them for their courage.

It tells others they are alive and
could use a little notice.

It affirms that you're glad
you still have them.

Listening, sharing, touching, laughing, celebrating,
can create a loving atmosphere for
your parents and
for you.

As you meet their needs,
your own needs may be met.

As you give them your hands,
you may find your own heart.

As you help them end their days,
you may find new beginnings in yourself.

For Further Help

Advocacy
The Gray Panthers
6342 Greene Street, Philadelphia, Pennsylvania 19144.

Education
Adult Education Association of the U.S.A.
1225 19th Street, Washington, D.C. 20036.

Emotional/Psychological Help
Family Service Association of America
44 East 23rd Street, New York, New York 10010.

Hearing
National Association of Hearing and Speech Agencies
814 Thayer Avenue, Silver Springs, Maryland 20010.

Homemaker Services
National Council for Homemaker–Home Health Aide Service
67 Irving Place, New York, New York 10003.

Nutrition
American Dietetic Association
430 North Michigan Avenue, Chicago, Illinois 60611.

Vision
National Association for the Visually Handicapped
305 East 24th Street, New York, New York 10010.

Nursing Homes
American Association of Homes for the Aging
529 14th Street, N.W., Washington, D.C. 20004.
        Represents nonprofit homes for the aging.

American Health Care Association
1025 Connecticut Avenue, N.W., Washington, D.C. 20036.

   Represents commercial nursing homes.

Rehabilitation
American Occupational Therapy Association
251 Park Avenue South, New York, New York 10010.

American Physical Therapy Association
1740 Broadway, New York, New York 10019.

Association of Rehabilitation Facilities
5530 Wisconsin Avenue, N.W., Washington, D.C. 20015.

Sexuality
Sex Information and Education Council of the
      United States (SIECUS)
1855 Broadway, New York, New York 10023.

Visiting Nurse Services
Visiting Nurses, National League for Nursing
10 Columbus Circle, New York, New York 10019.

Volunteer and Employment Opportunities
ACTION
806 Connecticut Avenue, N.W., Washington, D.C. 20525.

   FOSTER GRANDPARENT PROGRAM
   Serving children in pediatric wards,
   institutions for the mentally retarded,
   and facilities for the emotionally disturbed
   and physically handicapped.

   RETIRED SENIOR VOLUNTEER PROGRAM (RSVP)
   Offering involvement in public and nonprofit
   institutions.

SENIOR COMPANION PROGRAM
Helping adults with special needs
in nursing homes and other institutions.

SERVICE CORPS OF RETIRED EXECUTIVES (SCORE)
Retired business people provide management
advice to businesses.

National Council of Senior Citizens
1511 K Street, N.W., Washington, D.C. 20005.

National Council on the Aging
1828 L Street, N.W., Washington, D.C. 20036.

American Association of Retired Persons (AARP)
1909 K Street, N.W., Washington, D.C. 20006.